I0191551

Skies of Sea

AND OTHER POEMS

Chad Chisholm

Freedom's Hill Press

An Imprint of the Carolina Institute for Faith and Culture

Published by CIFC

Central, South Carolina

Copyright © 2021 Chad Chisholm

All rights reserved.

ISBN: 978-0-578-78846-3

ACKNOWLEDGMENTS

I want to thank those who have helped me with these poems or who have encouraged my career as a writer. I especially want to thank Mark L. Ridge and David P. Stubblefield— both of whom are more than colleagues to me. I want to thank Paul Shotsberger and Paul Schleifer for editing. I want to thank friends from Rust College, Margaret Delashmit and Sharron Sarthou; Lewis Knight, Steve Hayduk, and Tim Kirk from Southern Wesleyan University; Henry Gee who worked with me at *Mallorn* and Joseph Pearce at *Saint Austin's Review*. I also want to thank many dear people from my High School and University days: Lance, Joe, Aaron, Kevin, cousin Zac, and brother Brad. Finally, I am so grateful to my parents, Basil and Dana, for their patience, love, and guidance; I hope these poems honor them (and do not unduly embarrass them).

With the following exceptions, these poems are original to this volume: "Ode to Ginsberg" in *The South Carolina Review*, "Cardinal in the Storm" in *Connecticut Review*, "Orpheus Today" in the series *In Other Words*, "Southern Whitsunday" and "We Upward Walk" in *Saint Austin Review*, and "Orion's Final Song" in *The Mythic Circle*. The interview with Dr. Jonathan Sircy is reprinted with the kind permission of the Carolina Institute for Faith and Culture. The cover image is courtesy of Pixabay.

DEDICATION

For Grace and Lucy, my daughters—there is everywhere for you.

For Emily, my wife—Renoir you are.

TABLE OF CONTENTS

PART FOUR: FESTIVAL DAYS

CONVERSATIONS:

THE AUTHOR:

"If we shadows have offended,
Think but this, and all is mended—
That you have but slumbered here
While these visions did appear.
And this weak and idle theme,
No more yielding but a dream,
Gentles, do not reprehend.
If you pardon, we will mend.
And, as I am an honest Puck,
If we have unearnèd luck
Now to 'scape the serpent's tongue,
We will make amends ere long.
Else the Puck a liar call."

—William Shakespeare
From *Midsummer*

"But to have done instead of not doing
         this is not vanity
To have, with decency, knocked
That a Blunt should open
         To have gathered from the air a live
         tradition
or from a fine old eye the unconquered flame
This is not vanity.
         Here error is all in the not done,
all in the diffidence that faltered…"

—Ezra Pound
From *The Cantos*

Skies of Sea

AND OTHER POEMS

INTRODUCTION

Prelude to a Private World

FRIENDS who have favored me with reading and publishing these verses have asked that I include an overview of the ideas behind this book. Originally, I had reservations about providing an introduction because I think poems should stand for themselves without interference from an author; furthermore, readers have a right to an initial experience. However, those whose opinions I trust expressed concerns. For instance, one friend said, "Your poetry can be so counter-modernity, so neoclassicist, that people might not understand how to approach it." To address his concerns, I have taken a couple of steps: first, at the end of this book, I have included an interview I gave with Dr. Jonathan Sircy with whom I had a brief conversation before a keynote reading at a literary festival; second, I provided occasional notes to clarify some of the allusions and references; third, I am adding this introduction where I hope to contextualize some ideas that exhibit themselves throughout the book.

When I create an experience in poetic form, I am unaware of conscious attempts to refute modernist tenets concerning nature and creation, or to debate positivist principles regarding spirituality, and so on. As a poet, I'm unsure why some perceive me as anti-modern because my verses can feature mixes of modernist and traditionalist techniques. Ezra Pound and W.B. Yeats were as important to my poetic education as Shakespeare and Chaucer. Of course I have convictions and preferences, but I cannot compose a poem by setting down an abstract idea and then constructing a metaphysical artifice around it. Poems composed this way are artifacts for editors, and I find them devoid of interplay between poet, subject, and general reader. I never start with an abstraction; whether this admission commends or condemns my work, it is the honest truth.

In the Gospels, Jesus commanded us to love those whom he called "the least of these." In a paradox, we are told that the first will be last and the last will be first. However, a paradox of our modern culture is that those least in need of affirmation—wealthy celebrities, opinion influencers, protected political groups, social provocateurs, and so on—receive endless attention while those most deserving or in need of recognition receive the least. We see a similar inversion when contrasting what external sources tell us are 'important' things (for example, new commodities, celebrity snafus, political gaffs, symbolic signaling, and so on) with those things that provide us daily meaning but are never mentioned. The problem that comes from an inverted state of awareness is an old one, though it is intensified in our consumption-driven culture. However, our initial dissatisfaction can lead us to refocus our attention to ourselves and beyond ourselves, to those things closer to us and further from us, and so forth. When I read poetry, I am often turning my attention away from the trivial nonsense in our external world (the so-called "real world" according to those who either succumb to, hold authority over, or are able to influence it).

A return to what Edmund Burke called "the sublime" is often a historic reaction to such paradox. It is a form of spiritual recalibration for the soul where we once again choose to distinguish between vulgarity and beauty, falsehood and truth, or fleeting happiness and lasting joy. Throughout our history, poetry has called our attention towards what is worthy and good. When I choose to compose a poem, I am likewise searching for the sublime beyond the clouds of inversion. According to W.H. Auden, poetry has a lot to do with our choice of attention, and this calls us to consider choices we as individuals make on where to focus our consciousness. Auden said, "Choice of attention—to pay attention to this and ignore that—is to the inner life what choice of action is to the outer. In both cases, a man is responsible for his choice and must accept the consequences, whatever they may be."[1]

Auden's reference to an "inner life" of the poet features in my own work, and it bears some discussion. When a poet does share his or her private word, this serves a deeper purpose than a momentary change of mood. Henri-Frédéric Amiel, a Swiss philosopher, claimed that without an "inner life" individuals had little "resistance to circumstance." Amiel's argument about the 'inner life' confirms much of what I have learned and experienced these past few decades. He further elaborates that the person "who has no refuge in himself" exists "in the outer whirlwind of things and opinions":

> He who floats with the current, who does not guide himself according to higher principles, who has no idea, no convictions—such a man is a mere article of the world's furniture—a thing moved, instead of a living and moving being—an echo, not a voice. The man who has no inner life is the slave of his surroundings, as the barometer is the obedient servant of the air at rest, and the weathercock the humble servant of the air in motion.2

For me, what Amiel describes is at the heart of poetic philosophies and is also at the core of most of our great literary texts. If we lose ourselves, what else is there? This is a question that poets have addressed for a long time. In "Howl," Allen Ginsberg wrote that he witnessed "the best minds of [his] generation destroyed/ by madness," and as a professor and poet I have also seen what happens when individuals are driftwood on the tides of *zeitgeist*—how they are tossed about on wave after wave until being thrown aground to decompose on barren shores.

The poets are those who proclaim the dangers of conformity, of uniformity, of complacency, and so forth—movies and popular culture such as *Dead Poets Society* have made this a recognizable cliché. However, the idea that external forces need not determine who we become remains for me an incredible concept that has lost none of its potency. In "Self-Reliance," Ralph Waldo Emerson cautioned that "There are the voices which we hear in solitude, but they grow faint and inaudible as we enter into the world. Society everywhere is in conspiracy against the manhood of every one of its members." Then in his next paragraph, Emerson tells us, "Nothing is at last sacred but the integrity of your own mind."3 Some will object to Emerson's use of the word "sacred," and certainly what he says could be misconstrued as a defense for illiberal learning or nihilistic behavior. However, what Emerson conveys is that we as individuals should live from the inside and allow this to manifest itself in the outer world. In our modern culture, we tend to allow the external world to reign over consciousness and behavior. Emerson instead is contending that such a utilitarian approach for life is an inversion of how we were meant to live.

Of course, we cannot stop here. If we choose to be individuals whose inwardness of life will manifest itself in our outer world, then what we take into ourselves becomes more than a matter of private whims or peccadillos. As Emerson conveys, our minds must learn to foster integrity, and here the poets offer service. More than forms or craft, the private world of the poet is what matters. A longer conversation about poetic devices would be interesting, but general characteristics of poetry can be divided into four categories: heightened language, heightened consciousness, heightened discourse, and heightened reverence. Owen Barfield and others argue that the history of poetry chronicles the history of human consciousness because poetry as an act of human imagination helps cultures and peoples to create meaning at pivotal moments. Through its enhanced features, poetry is a cathartic experience for reader and poet: the two are codependent on each other, and both are transformed through these profound interchanges of heightened language.

At the very least, poets provide windows into their private musings and preoccupations, which has yielded undoubted inspiration and amusement for generations. At their best, poets give us a vision of the world both familiar and strange, an insight into the human mind that is comforting and disturbing, a moment in language that is amusing and terrifying. The great poems of the past seemed to simultaneously christen the consciousness of readers and lead them to new visions. Poems like *Beowulf* or "The Rime of the Ancient Mariner" appear to provide insight and catharsis when they are read outside of their eras. The Renaissance and Romantic poets often have answers for our dilemmas today, and Shakespeare asks us questions that we have forgotten how to ask ourselves.

If I have rendered no other service in this introduction, I hope I have been clear: the time has come for us to revisit our poetic ancestors. When we return after so long an absence, they will not expect an apology. Unlike media messaging or mass advertising that is relentless in its pursuit of our clouded attention, I find poets to be patient. When we want to return to a peaceful place and be receptive of truth and beauty, our poets throughout the centuries will always be present. They continue to wait upon us.

Notes:

1. Mrs. Humphry Ward (editor). *Amiel's Journal: The Journal of Henri-Frédéric Amiel* (London: Macmillan, 1885), p. 114.

2. Edward Mendelson, editor. *The Complete Works of W.H. Auden: Prose*. Volume VI. (Princeton University Press, 2015) p. 235

3. Ralph Waldo Emerson. "Self-Reliance." *The Norton Anthology of American Literature*. 6th ed. Eds. Nina Baym et al. New York, NY: W.W. Norton & Company, Inc., 2006. p. 541. Print.

Part One

Skies of Sea

Skies of Sea

For Lucy

1.
The mountaintop is a shore
Of World's End where we walk
And twilight leaves convert for you to colored glass.
Allhallowtide announces Carolina autumn
And sunlight sets below your feet
Upon the corridor cities.
Atop this sphere
The decline of days allows us
A gaze at Jupiter, the glowing disk;
Mars, the pale-red dot; Orion the Hunter;
Sirius and Procyon, the faithful dogs.
Lucy, you are one who knows
How to bathe face, hair, and feet
In seas of stars.

2.
The astronomy theater atrium
Decorated in 1950s sci-fi mementos
Is a galactic outpost with travel posters inviting us
To Europa or Olympus Mons.
The planetarium plays such features as
Oasis in Space, Exploding Universe, Chocolate Planet.
Aback you throw
Your head at painted space and stars
Glowing from the lobby's ceiling.
A Science Ed student scans our barcode;
Like a swimmer you tread and freestyle
Into the dome-shaped theater
On the ebb and flow of
Smooth and spatial ambient music

That seems at odds with Copernican Principle
Proclaimed throughout the movie.
So much more than others seated
You take in sights and sounds.
We witness the Big Bang, *Fiat Lux*!
You keelhaul tendentious talkers.
An indivisible fusion of awed delight
Can nevermore be blotted from so beaming a face!

3.

The film finishes, narrative fades
But cosmic art and music with us lingers
So after sunset we walk across the mountain
Led by red lights to an observatory reclining on a knoll
Peopled with stargazers and smaller telescopes.
They use iPhone apps to point lenses towards
The Pleiades, faint Uranus, or Orion's nebula.
Stars seem closer this time of year.
What could the Celts have known?
Do the boundaries between two worlds narrow?
Alexander Pope knew such thin places as these.
"All nature is but art, unknown to thee."

4.

The congregation of our cosmos tells of
The great and glorious (and occasionally good).
Sympathetic astronomers and science teachers
Take pains to point out to you
Princess Andromeda, Pegasus her rescuer,
And other constellations of autumn.
The rest of the *Clash of the Titans* cast is here—
Perseus, Cassiopeia, and Medusa (or at least her severed head).
I'm helpless with star maps—

Mere road atlases without lines or scale.
Yet no inhibitions freeze you from enticements.

5.
You are eight and dubbed autistic
But tonight no other stargazer will do.
You sprint in starlight for the knoll center
Stop before the dome-shaped building then
Snap around here and there—
Now peeking at a lens
Now peering at an iPhone augmentation
Raking in stars, planets, satellites, and discarded stage
boosters—
You scan them as a shelfed crab
Might seek out a sea cow overhead floating
Against a thalassic canvas of lavender and black.
Your heart need not stop for breath.
You cup both hands and reach
Into sheer airglow.

6.
Others see and smile—
To them you are a sea turtle gliding across
Tides and currents of starry skies.
They are not altogether wrong
For your mind, Lucy, is the marvel.
Whether astronomy or animals in recreated savannas
You see the cosmos in an aquarium
And the aquarist's tidiness in the cosmos.
Macrocosms and microcosms:
So exceptional are you to latch upon Nature's
economy—
Comet and clownfish each a part
Of a mutual menagerie.

7.
Beached upon a small mountain
Above cities we stand where
Tides of sky touch land and we can no further drift.
Each star is a saint to you applauding cosmic
commencement.
You are formed as stars and skies—
A marvel declining to explain itself.
Lodestars, meteor showers, and moon dust
Whisper in your attentive ear such verses
Lauding wonders you cannot touch with hands or feet
Unmeasurable mysteries few will ever know.
You find art in hallowed skies and become a hallowed
guide for me.
You are a hierophant for a humbled father
Who too often plays a doubting dupe, a despairing
drudge.
You show him wells of stellar waters from which you
drink
Teaching him a oneness beyond his words.

All Saints Night

I see what Dante meant
When he spoke of nature as art divine.
All the world is a cathedral lit in vesper light—
A star's handwriting on a page of hallowed skies.

We Upward Walk
For Lucy

We upward walk upon a hill
And see faces there in Carolina totality
Obscured by telescopes and welder masks.
Someone speaks into a microphone of gravity and light.
The westward gate holds blue hills and nothing beyond.
The movement of bodies above
The movement of bodies below
Are the same for those who downward look
And wonder if all existence (yours and theirs)
Is insalubrious or profane.
Much depends upon a soundtrack of life.
Rhythms of hills beyond
Move your soul to sudden dance.
Though Jacob's stairway is unseen
They see you sway and I wonder:
How can I teach them? What words can I use?
Teilhard de Chardin? "Nothing below is profane
For those who know how to see."

Then moon excuses itself before a star.
Two minutes pass. Faces cold as metal gaze
At something ripped from fabric sky—
A hole in the firmament hovers.
Stilled eyes and contorted minds
Rush through horrors of astrophysics
As a closed door is secured no longer.
Is there nothing in the dark?
In the midst of airglow they see you
Alone and autistic in pale umbra light
Cheering to embrace above a dark gemstone.
Then crescent sun restores the light.

As if a magician had finished his feat
Five-thousand who were silent applaud.
You say: "Solar Eclipse, again," and embracing laughter
Is the sole reproach for requesting an encore.

The microphone continues of gravity and light
As five-thousand follow down to the eastward gate.
They consider who commends a sun to moonward
dance.
Beyond us rhythms of hills whisper of an abiding where
we dwell
Among blue ridges, humbled and barefaced.
Striding behind your steps towards cars or careers
We upward walk assured that what we know is truer
Than what we vainly profess.

Where You Will Go

For Lucy

Dear Lu, Sweet Lu,
Lu of wild and daring ways—
How well I know
That you will go where you will go
In search of lands
Where men like elephants roam.
Dear Lu, Victor Lu,
Lu who whirls from stone to stone
Like an orange-chested robin
Among the petals of fig trees
Reminding all that you will go where you will go.
Come home, Lu, come home
From gales of sun
Where autumn spider-lilies are born
Before falling down to plant themselves
In the shade of houses and hickory.
Let us work harder
Let us find the ways
Let us work to set you free
So you can go where you will go.

Becoming Lilies

Yellow trumpet pitchers proclaim
At the gate an early Carolina autumn.
I walk along hardwood hedges
When in noontide sun I see
A lake or field of lustrous white lilies.
Along thick shrubs of turkey oak
I try for such a small glance of that sea of light
Or a hint of cicadas chorus
Singing of springtime and festival days.
At the end of hedges
I come to the edge of an open field
To see white flowers
Only to find stalks of hay
That in a sunbeam became lilies.
Resigned I could be, but I am not:
The yellow trumpets I pass again
Proclaim September's truth—
Beauty is beyond partition of particles,
And all life sings of unity within
Nature's unctuous integrity.

Christmas Eve Earthrise

Apollo 8 Mission

When we left home
Our Earth seemed old and arbitrated.
Whirling past lunar crags and canyons
Teeming newness becomes it—
A flaming blue dandelion through
The cracked pavement of space.
Domini est terra...

Theophany
Myth Retold

1.
From Lemnos and valleys of sun
I had come to Crete hearing legends
Of the young goddess who, freed from Delos,
Crowned in knotted moonlight,
Haunted islanders and hunted game.
In the agora, I found you
Searching stalls for figs and eggplants.
I could not trust newfound eyes:
How like a bumblebee you seemed astir,
Busy in fruit and vegetable beds
Holding peppers to your ears, onions to your chest—
Things that had no use for you, other than newness.
Tall as a tamarisk tree that hovers over huerta,
You were heads above sclerotic villagers
Who stared or fled the market.
You were unable to understand (for this I loved you).
You wandered to an apple stand
Towards a girl of nine or ten.
You kindly lowered your head
And offered her your hand.
You meant, I think, to give a kiss
When she took and bit your hand.
She saw you did not bleed and asked,
"Will you kill me?" "No," you said.
So wildly she ran away.
You did not understand (for this I loved you).

2.
We lived alone and hunted mornings.

Guineas and partridges were plentiful
Among leeward cliffs and amaranth blooms.
Afternoons we rested and loved.
No bowman was so calm or true,
Who in downpour could down a waterfowl.
One morning I said, "Leave the bow; fetch a spear."
We went upward into mountains to hunt boar.
Sirius and Procyon bayed ahead, and we came across
The fiercest of that wild sounder.
Behind his ears the dogs had him down.
We approached from behind;
Steady eye and hand, you sank spear between his ribs.
But something pierced your soul:
Archery, the passivity of quail or doves—
The kill was so close and sudden;
What was moving, struggling, threatening,
Emptied into a fruitless husk.
From a bowman's distance you never knew
How quickly all is forever changed.
Tears you cried, though not for him.
You held me. You held a moment back.
You held me close as you will hold me again.
Each embrace since, you hold me to hold a secret
Of loving well what soon you must let go.
And for this I love you.

Orion Beside Artemis

Myth Retold

1.
The late sunrise yawns languidly
To announce Sirius and Procyon
Will want a chase, a hunt, a stick of meat.
On impulse I glance for belt, bow, and bronze club
But thoughts and form reside with and beside you.
Thinning sheets around us warm;
Autumn leaves like stained glass in sunbeam
Fill our cabin windowsill.
There is a luminous chalice half-full
Of ambrosial mead brought with you and daybreak—
Again, I hear you say,
"From my father's house: take and drink."
What remains in the cup casts patterns of light
Upon darker parts of ceiling and the wall.
The remaining liquid is a seaside perfume
Floating from a three-legged bedside stool
Into amber tresses of your hair.
I see nothing complicated about your love—
Nothing but a gulf between mortality and you
Whose newness obscures how long
A life of forever can be
Whose newness conceals how weary
A life of deity will be.
In what houses of the dead shall we meet?
All there is echolalia and shadow.
Immortal damsel, what then is there?

2.
The ambrosial aroma of overnight hair

Compels me to consider each night
How you arrive at glowworm light
At bed with bread from Olympus tables.
Eventide toil and traversing cannot diminish
Your passion, virtue, or salvation that is you.
Pureness of beauty and thought—goddess to be,
You are a huntsman's hope for precious passing:
Each sunrise I'm met with unmerited returns
For love and hunts, much laughter, songs and prayers.
On these mortal ribs, this fading breastbone
Rest yourself and dream, dearest daughter of Zeus.
In you there is no scorn.
Happily you move in darkness
Taking no council with the night.
Upright you stand in the stronghold of Nyx:
You delight in valleys
Where trees and streams glow as stars.
No youth am I, but a selfish mortal huntsman:
A mere husk in the wind of Time. Shall I be
The cause of lonely condemnation
For one so wise yet unaware?
Is eternal wandering and despair for you?
Will I be a coward? Will I do it? Will I say it?
"Find thy kinsmen; be done with me.
Discard not thy divine beauty
Nor thine undying hope on one so doomed
To Hades and houses for the dead."

3.
The words remain unspoken.
Mortal nature again surrenders
To the gracious passion that is your gift
And I feed upon your penultimate love
Which is will, deed, and pleasure of trust.

When you seek my shade in Hades
Will I know you? Respond to entreaties? Reassure you?
Can mortal dead comfort those who live and never die?
Still closed, I see the cerulean silver of your eyes
Plead with a form, a shell—a helpless echo
That remonstrates not against the darkness to proclaim
Glory, honor, and praise that here I sing.

4.
Then shift you, smile and settle again against
My restlessness so that now
I see a limitless secret kept within your sleep:
All seems ambrosial—the chalice, your hair, you.
Despite the rage of a twin brother because
Of habitual lateness at nightfall
The sun dances around your unguarded borders
Spawning medallion colors around the room.
What substance—ichor and ethereal—has for me
become veined?
What whispers hear I of the passing of Nyx's offspring?
Death will cease to exist? What gift is this?
No outcomes I see, but love I mortal things
As can an immortal, O daughter of gods!
Newness of thoughts, reason, passion beset me!
I grasp through soul and senses a togetherness
In stars beyond stars, huntsman and goddess made new
Beyond the firmament, beyond the dawn.
Artemis, O Artemis: mercies of all mysteries—
Divine canvas for mortality; beloved woman and
betrothed deity;
Together in all spheres, all shared eternities.

Orion's Final Song

Myth Retold

Artemis, Mavourneen:
Once more to touch your moonlit hair.
I say someone beautiful as you
Hardly understands the life whirling about you
Sealing minds and tongues of hunters
But, as wildflowers among weeds,
Hold high your heads and bloom
Not indifferently, but oblivious to things sublunary
Mad with Nyx's nympholeptic storm
(And all other such seeming-silliness)
Rushing and rolling, beveled and unable to offend.

Artemis, Mavourneen:
Tears I feel for me? No mortal form is immune.
Water no more Scorpio's arrows and stings:
There's always another star above.
Cry for the sea, Gaia's most mewed and ancient lover:
Wild, hopeless, and immortal Oceanus
Restless chancellor of a thousand colonies;
Pitiable kinsman, he rages perpetually
Towards the moon and sandy mainland.

Artemis, Mavourneen:
Yet see you will, or…see you now?
As a Delos girl on an April day
Could you see flocks of seagulls and jaybirds
Fluttering through a bushel of chrysanthemums?
Did you listen to wingtips waving above
Fragrant buds, from petals both lithe and fresh?
And did your cerulean eyes in childhood

Become vaporous and vein red?
And did your newness of heart then know
The birds and blooming buds
(Through no fault of their own)
Could never know nor comprehend
What still you feel like flocks of quail flushing
Through reeds beneath your breastbone?
Weep you still those nonage tears?

Artemis, there is your heart.
Mavourneen—there is your heart!
Goddess to be: there is your heart.

Note: While there are different stories about the death of Orion, the inspiration for these poems mainly comes from Hesiod's *Astronomia* where the huntsman Orion comes to Crete for the wild game and there becomes the beloved of Artemis, goddess of the moon and the hunt. Orion and Artemis became hunting companions, and the mortal huntsman won the heart of the young immortal. However, their love was short-lived. Because of his zeal for the hunt as well as his boasting, Orion angered Gaia, the primordial goddess of the Earth, who then sent a gigantic scorpion to battle the famous hunter. While Orion fought valiantly, he fell mortally wounded. When he died, Artemis was devastated by the loss of her only love. According to most legends, Artemis pleaded with Father Zeus to engrave Orion's image in the skies as a memorial to the great huntsman, and he honored her request. As a mature goddess, Artemis never took another lover but remained celibate and became a protector of maidens, hunters, children, and expectant mothers.

Part Two

Ordinary Times

Who
Green Man's Return

Who's he
Who makes
Woods sound
Of rainwater?
Who roods
Wind and pinwheels?
Who puts
Pen to paper?
Who cleanses
Thoughts whole?
Who?

Note: The Green Man (also known by other names such as The Leaf King or The Old Man of the Woods, and so on) is a mysterious, leafy-headed spirit who is often a symbol of renewal. While it is believed that the Green Man originated from pre-Christian culture, many churches are decorated with carvings and windows of this ancient figure.

Ode to Ginsburg

For your rebirth into the glorious machine
Never underestimate
The starry significance of
A red pen.

Theory Seminar

He said, "theory is all literature,
Cause stories and people would be obscure
Without it." He didn't blink or
Strain and couldn't search anymore,
Screened from blooms of blue because he was "sure."

Only Renoir

For Emily

Twenty years and I'm too diffident to declare
That I see Renoir in you. Should I try?
I imagine a rare childless summer afternoon
You applying sunblock around a black swimsuit—
One that gleams like salamander skin when wet—
And laughing the moment I say,
"Emily, you are Renoir."
You repine a glance, then proceed to rebuke teasingly:
"Oh, those *fat* women." Face-to-face I'm too awestruck
For some Renoir repartee, but reduced
To an attendant to finish off sunscreen
For parts unreachable—then you depart
For white sand and gulf waves.
And I see Renoir.

Too close to an artist's ideal are you
So he could only capture you in segments.
Three Bathers you are in the middle
Holding the brunette with one hand
And teasing her with a live crab in the other.
Two Girls at the Piano and *In the Meadow*,
You wear rosewood pink and Renoir has
The brown cherries of your hair.
Then the *Two Little Circus Girls*:
Your hands in air, feet surrounded by oranges for
juggling;
Then legs together, hugging oranges like a blanket;
One minute opening your body, the next
Being brave before men with circus glasses.
But Renoir's *Portraits* (all of them) have your eyes:

Mere embankments of whole universes
Glowing beneath clothes, hair, and skin.

Twenty years ago in London I stood before *La Loge*
(An older couple wanted to look around me)
Considering how memory conflates taste and image;
But Renoir with the lady creates synesthesia—
She is a cream whose flavor changes
With objects on and around her.
The gold railing—banana;
Her opera glasses—cream soda;
Her lipstick—cranberries;
Her pearls and diamonds—ice cream;
The two corsages—strawberries and sherbet;
The two vertical stripes—a chocolate truffle.
Ageless I call you, but have you traveled time?

Renoir's bouquet shades the bland
Backgrounded man preoccupied with binoculars.
From my old 1989 Mustang I saw you
With a friend in a parking lot beneath
The overpass outside the (mostly bad) comedy club.
I see you still in dark blouse and pink pants
A symbioses of shyness and serene naturalness:
And my soul, a kite, reaching for cloud.
I am this bland man beside you—
Like Samuel Johnson, "dull" or distant,
"Not delightful." A "harmless drudge"
Who "busies himself" with words.

To Renoir you give life. You are Renoir.
But could I be your background man?
Braved from shadows, might you favor me?
Is there flavor enough in an eclipsed face for you

To teach me to fail yet flow, to let go but not forget?
You do well in all weathers,
But are most made for sun and bright skies.
You are belladonna of the banquet hall,
But your habitat is meadow or Mediterranean coasts.
You redeem a life too inwardly rooted—
You, Emily, are salvation to words: my words.
Behold, Renoir you are—one and only.

Out of Season

Apocalyptic Tale

I stopped, wiped my face, lit a cigar, and
Saw a dead doe, its receding carrion
Formed a modeling smile. I finished and
Skipped the butt inside her ribcage and
Hiked on below. I was a trespasser,
But I felt boss of those trees. I hiked six
Ridges over and stopped to rest on one
Overlooking the creek. Along came what
I thought a doe, which stretched its neck and drank.
Ka-prow. All too easy. I blew into
Its left eye. I went below, approached it
Carefully: its socket was like a coal
I'd stirred, but closer I saw pubescent
Antlers sprouting forth, mere virgin noggins.
On his coat were faint white spots. With boulders
I propped him on his back. Him being young,
I didn't need my hatchet, and used my
Army machete to slash his neck and
Genitals and, when he'd bled enough, cut
Along his midline. I used my hand to
Hold back his paunch and intestines, and split
The pelvis point. The day grew hot so I
Quickly stripped him, chopped and wrapped each round in
Cheesecloth, fit him economically and
Discretely inside my pack, left his skin,
Head, offal, and re-hiked the six ridges
Back where I began. I needed rest from
My load and wanted a second cigar.
The squirrels and birds were as before, but I

Saw, before I pitched my butt, the blood of
The dead doe running near my boots, freshly.

Jocassee's Heartbeat
Green Man's Return

Driving cavalierly fast
O'er narrow upland roads
Praying to clash like Gettysburg, or overload.
And for him that will be all. Instead he's at the lake
Beveled betwixt the lowlands
And the blue shadowed ridge,
The water clovering the bank
Making hunched shoulders into fat land fingers.
He hikes four coves
O'er dead banked trees
Passing cheery redneck children,
Redneck parents and their rancid dogs
While tripping stupidly
O'er man-deposited concrete and lime rock,
Then on the second cove he views more
Of Charles' northland where clouds brood
Casting some shadows while other peaks
Are free like he to tan.
He reaches his cove, the fourth, deserted, with a tiny
waterfall
Where nature shares its own libation
And rolls and twists a goblet rock
Into a shape as a water nymph's divan
And in swim trunks he sits, scoots, and reclines
Into its cool, watercress cushion.
Ready for the lake,
The unvanquished warm and cool currents
Of the Keowee, Whitewater, and Thompson Rivers
Are an orbing chrism around and o'er him, lowering his
heartbeat.
From cove to cove he swims de Gamaly.

After six coves he's against the mountains' cleft,
Content for now to rest and wade-walk like Dias here.
Gettysburg can wait while he's wodwo of the lake.
O to be the air that coats the ridges and their rills.
To never need food, to never worry of betrayals:
To ride streams and mountains and live only
Day to day to stir crags and clouds.

The Chandelier

For Pawpaw

Ole boy, I was in Berlin
And going home the first wave
When my CO said I had to stay.
Wasn't all bad. Got a Mercedes.
But they stuck me in an empty hotel
In a bombed block.
It stood like a church in that rubble.
Bored, I drank a lot.
Long before the Russians had looted
Anything worth a damn,
But this chandelier, wide as the lobby.
On the couch I started staring,
And there was nothing doing,
So I took out my forty-five
And shot the damn thing up
Until I heard a knock.
At the stairway door was a GI, saying,
"You under attack?"
I never knew he was upstairs,
The area bombed and all.
Stupid, I could a blown his foot off.
Me and Wayne, that was his name, became friends,
And he helped me.
We only could take
Four hundred dollars to the States.
I had forty hundred
From selling cigarettes to the Russians.
Wayne took some money and found others,
So when I came back here
Mother said, "You made bunches of friends,

Twenty letters from Detroit, Chicago, New York."
All but a hundred dollars!
See, if I hadn't acted a fool
And started shooting that chandelier
I'd never a met Wayne.

The Raccoon's Cue

For B. and L.

Late, hot, and dark, he knew his time
And had little to fear from stupid humans
Who mixed libations with firearms.
Too inebriated to sleep, we cut and were eating
Watermelon (of all things) when he came
Cracking leaves like Christmas paper.
He froze in flashlight wincing copper beneath his eyes.
Someone fired eight rounds! Pistols were illegal!
We killed the lamp, ran for bags,
And you tripped and cut your hand on something
sharp.
All night you swore, "I killed that raccoon!"
"Bulls-t," we said. "It's laughing its tail off at you."
"You'll see," You declared. "I killed it dead!"
I dreamed of the childhood we shared,
Performing the vice-actor minutes before.
We'd beat and beat each other and sometimes laugh
And sometimes feel such shame. Why did we do it?
I must have slept like King Richard
Under the Arkansas stars,
Dreams heavy with thoughts of school and college.
But morning came and, moaning off whisky,
We found the cooler, ten feet off, open.
With a bandaged hand you showed me
The rest of the watermelon:
A husk scratched clean.
We three laughed.
"I missed him, brother."
"I guess so."

Display Case

For Lucy

"Some of us are here to teach!"
Wow. It's hard to conceal anger
Within a school atrium
Inside their no-man's-land
Between two doorways—
One door is near offices of school staff
And another bars your way
Towards dreams of rolling hills
Crowned in golden blue.
I sit on a bench that faces a glass case
With another official who discusses
Your suitability for school.
Can I put a human face on a Spreadsheet?
Lady Macbeth could see
Her father's face on Duncan's sleeping body,
But could anyone do likewise
On a school behavioral report?
The same conversation,
The same words politely dissembled:
We like Lucy, but it's our parent base here—
Professors and administrators at a research university.
Away I drift and watch you wonder
Around the display case
To gaze at plaques and self-promotion:
All conspicuous displays of virtue and caring.
The administrator continues:
Think of how busy our parent base is…
I see the busyness of these people—
Building model bridges in their basements
Or digital tunnels in their garages

Projects that are never built,
Designed for the sake of endowments and money
From government and private industry.
My war of thoughts stop for a moment
At an image in the display case
That shows you and a classmate with autism.
(Interesting how your image appeared
One week before you transferred out.)
Also our parent base is well-paid,
And their mortgages are so high,
And they expect…no that's not quite right…
She has to say but she cannot say it:
These parent professors demand
That their lives not be complicated
With inclusive instruction
Or accommodating children like you.
They don't remember they work in education
Because they don't what to hear
Your excitement in a nearby room
When you learn something new.
Somewhere in the drumroll of unsaid words
You wander over to the display case.
Besides, our parents have expectations:
Indeed, they do—
They expect six-year-olds in twelve years
To earn a full-ride into Ivy Leagues,
Medical school, engineering school, biotech school.
The woman ceases to speak;
I cease to pretend to listen.
In front of us we hear
The slide door opening.
Neither of us knew the display case
Was unlocked until you opened it.
It's interesting because

You leave me to wonder,
Who is the teacher and who is the learner?
You are here for those of us
Too proud and stubborn to learn.
That could tell us something about your purpose.
You are here to teach.

The Flittermouse

Invader of our parish mass
A churchgoer without class
You use our altar for an outhouse
And make our carpet contain your trash.
And of course you brought your spouse
And of course you brought your cubs together
Seeking sanctuary from wet weather
And now our altar space and rails are doused
In batty excrement, and our nave that
Has become your cave and habitat.
So we worship in the fellowship hall
As we wait evicting lifts and slats
While in our church you have a free-for-all
You unwelcome family of bats!
You are something birdlike without a feather—
But for a moment if we could tit for tat
Perhaps the reason I do not like you, bat,
Is because your name cannot compensate
For an ominous form or for the rouse you make.
Or your reputation to chouse
Our church sexton or parish handyman.
Yet how I love the word "flittermouse"
Because of the picture it helps me scan
Of furry fliers comforting those in a jailhouse
Or a fun and playful pet for the picnic
Only to snatch a deviled egg on a double-quick.
So remarkable that this could be the cure
The power of words and nomenclature.
Flittermouse, I so wish you well
And when you leave (for more, I hope, than a spell)
I pray you find a more harmonious place to dwell.

The Tree

Requiescat in pace

In another life
You, Ted Hughes, and I walked together
And stopped beside a Devon tree
Standing solitaire, used by cows for shading in summer,
And a marker for sheep to pasture away.
It was tall, tight, and thick,
And hardly echoed when I knocked.

Ted, how do trees grow?
You answered: outwardly on my farm.
But Ted, how about the inside?
No, you said lowering your bristled brows,
That's just dense deadwood.
Does it mean anything for the tree? I pleaded.
No, the deadwood supports the tree,
But it's a grounded stick without
The vascular outer rings.
For awhile you went into the dark woods
And left me by my tree.

Attrition wore you all,
And one by one you went—
Larkin, Hughes, Ammons—
Along with you dead poets
Who would be dying—
Lowell, Bishop, Plath, Berryman,
Jarrell and Sexton,
Snodgrass and Justice.
Ever such truths in lies again?

When you returned with your rake and barrow
Filled with old fall's leaves and limbs, I asked:
Ted, will this tree die?
Yes Ted, I know most generations
See the ashes
Brighter than the phoenix.
But this tree has grown
So wide
And the outer rings are stretched
So thin.

Highway Overpasses

Loneliness comes
In sounds at twilight
Like the serenading of
An invisible solitary cricket in a lot
Beneath assertive penumbra
Of a highway overpass.

Ordinary Times

Red leaves seen
On blueberry boughs
Declare an end
Of times between.
Nature's patterns
Recall such scenes
Of June clatter
Of catbirds and waxwings.
Warblers and finches
Sing austere songs
Of cold riches
And autumn gone;
Of harvest climes
And ordinary times
Now done or dead.
A mosaic of red
Formed from hundreds
Of blueberry leaves
(Some on pavement
Some on trees)
Arranged together
Proclaim a center
Rebirth within:
A manifestation
Of mind and breath
Signaling a death
Of ordinary times.

Part Three

Isles Before Palms

Orpheus Today
Myth Retold

Hell almost resembles
The Blue Ridge Mountains, drying; drying
And the river smells and feels of
Old spilt beer.

The damned are shoeless
Yet their teeth are tight,
Whiter than
Their albino cheeks.

In this sunless, starless space
Orpheus strings and sings of
The only thing
He knows for truth:
His heart, bleeding openly.

Yet for all his summoned
Love and passion
The damned
Cannot, will not, understand.

Isles Before Palms

I dream of green palms
Waving in wind and sunlight.
So long at sea, so very long—
A featureless gray mass
Forever moving and moving
That never seems to move.
I see land and rejoice!
But these tidal lands are flat
Uneven chains of sand.
There is no welcome here
Or handwave of green
For these are isles
Before the palms.

The Motorist

Memento Mori

The motorist had seen rood markers
Along the roads, and dead deer too; but finally today
Off a hard Carolina hook of a highway curve
He pulls on the left shoulder with red-eyed cars
And follows many into a woody median.
Passing a man on an iPhone,
He smells anti-freeze and oil without unction
Before seeing the jeep with a New Jersey tag—
A car pelted around the wrong way,
Crushed by a head-on hit from a hickory.
It smells of smoke and dust;
No skid marks, no second car.
They encircle the warm meteor and gaze.
Death walks and day wilts to paleness.
A woman tries opening the driver's door.
The iPhone man screams, "Wait for the ambulance!
For God's sake, wait for the ambulance!"

The motorist sees the driver at twenty feet.
Probably his age, but the crash
Carved and converted her human head
Into a shape like a shark's, but not the sea prowess:
Against the headrest her broken neck
Was like a dead one, lying on a lab table
Belly up and crushing its own dorsal fin.
All look but eyes dare not wait upon smudged jaw and
forehead.
It seems impossible that one eye or organ lived,
But the lower lip moves as if pulled by
A ghostly ventriloquist not quite jettisoned.

Another woman listens, but he cannot hear.
For a second, her eyes pull at him.

The motorist walks back to the shoulder
Allowing no forces charge over him.
The woman at the driver's door cries: "For Christ's
sake,
Are they coming? Are they coming?"
The vision, for the motorist, is wasted.
Behind rood markers something for him is hidden:
For him they are misleading, their memories selective.
Hours pass as he drives, trying to leave her
With the white lane-lines, her mouth and jaw.
Shadows grow between the trees, so on he flips
His headlights and then remembers
A brim fish he'd caught with his uncle.
The motorist always removed hooks cleanly,
But once it was deep: so he grabbed it,
And made a cracking branch-sound.
The greatest horror was neither sound nor blood,
But with half its jaw hanging off it couldn't scream:
The only proof of pain was its erect serrated fin.

The motorist will dream of flowery roods
So he can forget. And on he drives into the cast
Of eventide with no faith to make him well.

The Wisteria Tree

I walk from work
To find a toiled tree
Covered with wisteria.
The invasive woodwork
Stands sixty feet high.
Its feathered leaves
Obscure the genus of the tree.
Sunbeams vanish in twining weaves
And all beneath dries or fades.
Lavender teardrops conceal stems
That clockwise twist the bark.
All is enmeshed in spidery mayhem.
Scented poison grows in shades.
It is a wisteria tree.

Señor Candyman

Distant highway montanas block the way
To Cancun, Veracruz and Mexico City.
With the autobus, now people pass
And do "bible work" inside recluse pueblos
Sealed in valley-pockets like gnomes.
The village seemed deserted; all seemed quiet
When two boys were told to take "Easter" candy bags—
Shelled-sugar with lemon food coloring—
From the cool trailer and into arid heat.
"When the kids come, give 'em two pieces each!"
They waited until someone clanged an old bell;
From nowhere they came—What's the difference
Between a thousand and a million? They came upon them.
Mas caramelos, por favor! The work was slow, sticky, and hot.
From all sides, the boys were pelted down.
How to escape? One boy recalled a Christmas candy rain.
"Hey, check this out." He grabbed two handfuls of candy
And threw them different directions, slow pitch,
Trying to make a path: The boys saw heads
Open like cans on rock and pebbles.
Most were up like bowling pins, but a couple could not.
Glugging sounds from moist, jagged craters
Echoed across the Sierra Madre Orientals.
The smell of blood, lice-sweat, yellow candy-slobber
Mixed with high altitude topless-dirt, cried out the crime.
"We weren't told. We didn't mean this."
"There were too many. What do we do?"
The only answer was the choking
Of skinny-stray dogs behind barbwire.

Grayscale

For those whose love
Can lead them into dreams of grayscale.
Such peace that I can offer
Go with you, my kindred friends.
Your love is never in vain.

1.
Long ago,
In a nightmare world
In tones of gray
Trancelike I led you
Onto a flatbed truck
Where other children
(Who couldn't interact
Or "pitch-in"
Or put "mission first"
Or be "efficiency tightwads")
Held the stakebeds.
You are always three
And can't say much.
You eye me, smile and say,
"Bye-bye, Daddy."
When resurrected
From moral or malignant spell
I see your eyes
Alight like diamond valleys
Of September autumn.
You cannot see danger.

2.
I want to shake you.
Desperate, I plead.
I want you to live!
I cannot grasp you.

You stand still
On the truck
But like air, you elude—
I cannot overcome
That lilting look
Of autistic invincibility.
Then grayscale barricades
And off the flatbed goes.
Your look never leaves.
Your ghost smile remains
After the flatbed disappears
Into darker forests.

3.
Eyes and voice
From grayscale lands
Echo across seven years.
Today downstairs
I hear you as I pack
For the facility.
Perhaps for a month?
You don't know.
Across the street
Outside our windows
Is a red maple
Beneath evergreens—
I acknowledge but cannot see:
All is grayscale.
I want to see
A girl of ten
With father, mother, sister:
It fades to facelessness
Of grayscale.

4.
A rolling suitcase
Is full of clothes,
Plush dolls, and nostalgia.
I fetch an heirloom—
My grandmother's book
Full of favorite poems:
Aloud, I hope
Someone will read them.
How to let you go?
Before I'm done
You go outside.
I find you
On the trampoline
In nimbus sunglow.

5.
Wildly away, you
Bounce final moments
Colliding with things
Neither can see
But barrage about us.
Then suddenly upward
Clutched in vacuous currents
You float like debris
Laced in radium, launched
Towards a void:
My soul is scythed
Into such hells
Of grayscale.

The Rat

The rat after hours
Climbs rain gutters
Enters the delicatessen
Underneath aging twilight;
Enters kitchen from
Collied ceiling light.
Inverted on rafters
Spies a cold fryer,
Copious with fragments
Surfaced on his snare.
Sensing manna,
Jovially he lunges
For a swim and swells
Himself to drown.

The Siren Queen

Myth Retold

With mead on their lips, and treasure laden
To their ship, the sailors with a full mast
Rippled the sea. Poseidon was annoyed
But tolerant if they stayed "on the roof."
Their square sail filled, they raced home singing old
War songs. Their waves crashed against the island.
Teles, the Siren Queen, side-stepped wet stones
In her silks. An emerald ring winced on her
Middle toe. Her lady warned her about tides
But Teles wore it, a gift from Nereus
Said to soothe blood and calm the heart. She heard
Singing before the mast filled the horizon.
The stirred waves stained her silks and stole her
Ring, covering its shine with sands and weeds.
Teles swept across the stream bank and found
The Sirens asleep, their slumber warmed
By rinses of sunrise and seagull song.
"Awake," Teles cried, "Or I'll be ravished!"
"Please, my Queen. Let us sleep for the second
Crow." Like a rabid mountain goat she cried:
"At your feet! Guard my dignity which pleads!"
Drowsy, they formed crooked arcs on the rocks
Facing the ship sailing north of the island.
Some reflected on Nyx who left Chaos
To initiate a procession for
The Sirens: a post for ceremony
Master was made, Teles chosen as queen;
The throne wearied all with threats and questions.
The sailor's songs flowed overboard waking
The Sirens, and their hearts grew with their eyes.

They sang their youth to wish-off the vast air.
The ship changed course and crashed into the rocks.
From the far bluff Teles watched her Sirens
Ruin their silks to pull young sailors ashore.
She twitched watching the girls wipe salty water
From the boys foreheads, lips, and stony eyes.
"They're hurt," said the Sirens. "Let us care for them."
The Queen called the kelp to drag the sailors
Into the sea. They wailed; the Sirens wept.
Poseidon shook and quaked the deep to free
The uninvited sailors from his sea.
As the waves gashed the rocky isle, the Queen
And her Sirens ran for the highest ground.
The sea shook with fury, but the kelp held.
"My sea shall be cleaned," declared Poseidon,
"Even if I must drown the entire isle."

Spider Poems

Fat and long-legged, not moving much
In her quiet quest to build a novel web
Shaped like a stop sign
                    In the window.

In the center she stores her silk
And weaves an inner-castle that heavies
                    The thin outer ribbons.

I'd love to whack it all
Or slash her mass and free
All that tortured blood, but no.

Behind are leafy boughs
Like little hatchet fingers that
                    Await the coming wind.

Always Evaporates

The cold pot of stagnant water
On my stove is an experiment on *pathos*.
I ignited the burner to prove
That water would boil effortlessly
Over the rim into unchained malice.
It did! And it would always evaporate
Leaving the pot sterilized for later use.

Come on, John
Requiescat in pace

Come on, John: has it been so long?
How to compose a eulogy?
A macaw in a polar sun?
A penguin in tumescent tropics?
Nothing works, so I drive to old spots—
The closed putt-putt course,
The boarded video arcade,
The card and sports memorabilia shop—
Looking for some sign of you. I cannot find it.
To baser uses these things return.
But somewhere, somehow you live
In memories of card trades where you won
Not for shrewdness but for sheer audacity,
Offering a Saints' rookie for Pete Rose.
How could we help it? You had no inhibitions:
At putt-putt there was a curvy girl
Sheathed in a dress of moon-silver;
None of us approached her, but you did.
(She was closer to our age than yours.)
"Hey sweets! Play a few holes? I bet you'll laugh."
Twenty years ago, I remember her smile
As we watched her careen ahead with you.
There were your West Coast witticisms
That charmed the most humorless Mississippi enclaves
As well as songs, jokes, talk of football games,
Rock bands from a time before;
Recitations of Poe, Hawthorne, and Whitman,
Arguments over Hemingway and Kerouac.
Conversations about classic guitarists—
Always, I was able to flummox you

Ranking Hendrix below Brian May.
You countered I could never play guitar like you,
And my repartee was to tease your verses:
"If Shelly were a nightingale
Then Ginsberg a crow should be.
How now, America...How now..."
How I now have these near-illegible lines
Tucked into your Allen Ginsberg anthology,
I am unsure. Your book is well-used,
But I only glance to remember you.
You were a poet if not with words.
Where are you now? Somewhere? Nowhere?
That is not quite true.
You live in me. You are part of me.
Come on, John—it has been so long.

My Neighbor's Tree

Beside his house
My neighbor planted a tree
That had grown too close.
So at springtime he asked me
To hold elastic chords
To pull it down and shift its fall
Away from the air and heat machine
As he used a handheld saw.
Though the tree seemed a solid statue,
With schools, shops, and museums closed
There was nothing to do.
I held chords behind waist and knees
While he climbed his ladder.
The tree belonged beside a sea.
Today it had to die.
I watched him on a ladder in his red vest
Sawing and pushing at bark
And he seemed to make no progress.
I wanted to reconsider
The soundness of such plans
But I had become involved.
But after enough sawing and pushing
I felt the tree weaken in my hands.
The parish bells were ringing
Though I knew no one was there.
Before it cracked and began swinging,
It fluttered to demurely ask,
"What have you done?" Am I sure?
Within chains and reins of circumstance
My neighbor planted a tree
And I helped him rip it down.

How mysterious our actions seem to be.
Nothing left to ponder but this irony.

Henpecked Diogenes

For A., friend and philosopher

I asked Coors' infrastructure why he chose
To stay, Eros aside. He said "Duos
      Suffer since there's nowhere to go,
      But trust showed the light I know."
I said "You think every thorn has a rose?"

Time Storm

Rolling waves
Of clouds
At twilight dawn
Gust on heads
Of porch-lit houses.
Autumn leaves
In whirling mists
Are the corners
Of a wheeled pawl—
Yellow, green, and red
They cleave
Against branches
Until time when
Like marbled powder
Down they come
In spiraling swells
From bulbs above
To carpet
Piedmont soil.
Houses sleep
As tidal sky
Looms in wait
Of dawn.

Cardinal in the Storm

The short and loblolly pines bend in the wind
Clouds spread like a spider web
To stir the sky and jettison their cargo.

He comes from the forest, a red bolt,
And, like a lord, perches on the seed bucket
Hanging off the elm.

I'd warn him: *My wife's gone, and*
The feeder's more full of shells than seeds.
But can only witness, like a ghost, while

The rain heavies his red wings. Like a lion
He holds his chest, furiously scraping shells out
Among leaves and limbs dropping to the ground,

Till he finds it, displays it in his beak
For me to see (like Moses on the mountain)
And bolts back into the forest.

Lighthouse

Between highway lanes
      Biloxi's lighthouse rests
Above palms maintaining
      Greenness in cold repress.
Into sunset I hope to go
      And ascend stairs to address
What Heraclitus said (that "all is flux")
      Against a westward glow.
Trust needs truth, and truth wants trust.
      So I'll climb these spirals to see
(So bright, a source of light)
      The bay below, the goldstone sea.

Above stopping traffic, I found
      A man passing the crosswalk
Moving towards the Mississippi Sound.
      A thousand rippled suns block
The automated headlights below.
      He moves and cannot look
To see his way: but on he goes,
      His red jacket and white shoes
Disappearing towards sea so smooth.
      Each step for him is as it should:
Truth is trust and trust is truth.
      The path is even, paved, and gold—
Difficult to see; never misunderstood:
      Immutable belief in timeless mold.

The Dionysus Tree
Myth Retold

1.

Away from frenzied festivals
You lead me to visions of old Grecian sunlight.
There we traverse vineyards.
Our shadows point towards the solitaire Thracian tree
That shades cows in summer
And is a marker for sheep to pasture away.
It feels tight and stubborn as serrated rock
And does not echo when I knock.

2.

You are Dionysus, lord of the grape-harvest:
I ask, "How do trees grow?" You answer, "Outwardly."
I ask, "Tell me about the *inside*?"
You lower bristled brows and say,
"No, that's just dense deadwood."
"Does it mean anything for the tree?"
"No. Deadwood supports the tree.
It's a grounded stick without outer rings."

3.

You drift with cool Hellenic breezes into dark woods
And leave me beside the tree
To remember when we were young:
They called you "He Who Comes."
Now you seem threadbare and old.
Attrition has worn your poets and their songs:
Homer with his regal splendor; then Hesiod,
The lonely and impoverished farmer
Who taught me to live a good and worthy life.

And then Aeschylus, Pindar, and Sophocles—
Our country buries them before their words are spent.
Ovid and others are clever, but not reverent—
They denude our myths of meaning, transforming them
Into idle tales for idle people:
"Monstrous lies never seen by human eyes."

3.
Here is no fertile Alexandra or lustrous Rome.
These vineyards are carved from
Rocky paths below and stony hills above.
Poets abandon Greece as she abandons them.
The purple narcissus is more comfortable
On the Nile's lower banks in view of the Pharos.
The red anemone—windflower of Adonis—
Is better planted beside the Tiber and Rubicon.
Yet among these crevices and crags is this tree.

4.
You return with rake and bundle
Filled with leaves and limbs from last autumn.
I do not turn to look. I ask instead,
"Will the tree die? It has grown so wide, its roots
shallow,
Its soil too hard, its outer rings stretched too thin."
Then from deep despair I was amazed—
You stood a youth, radiant in Olympian glory.
Instead of rake you held a thyrsus braided with lilies.
I feared my death, but with such tacit kindness
You reassured me of the salvation of Semele,
Beloved queen and your mortal mother.

5.
"See it is not so," you said. "Behold the tree."

With something more strange than earth or firmament
The tree was not a tree
But something formed of divine smithcraft.
Old winter leaves rustled underfoot
Beneath a spirit aglow in tree-form.
You stood before such dewy leaves
Lilting in goldstone dawn to declare,
"I am twice-born Dionysus. All who love me
Love well those works of hands and heart.
Leaves and flowers come in time and go in time,
But the tree has truth and truth is the tree
And for all who love for more than me
So will its honor and glory ever be."

Part Four

Festival Days

Southern Whitsunday

Old Saint Paul's is a timeworn egg
Feathered in an oaken nest:
Quite the solemn landmark.
Beleaguered by stones marked for old Carolina names:
A memorial for the wistful.
Inside are candles seldom used.
The stained window above the altar is crossed and
crowned:
Words in letters gold and black declare "The Lord is in
his Holy Temple."
Is it so? Is it a dream?
Were you there?

Yet Old Saint Paul's is a stage:
Two rooms for a perceptive audience.
Blue hallowed light unveils a side room
And like Great Pepper's Ghost all is transformed.
Through the mystic plate of glass
A world of sweat and muscadine blossoms is revealed:
Sunshine and the smells of barns (both pleasant and
less so)
Fill the barren nave, pour forth from the sacristy.
Boots for alfalfa and palms for canned preserves fill the
pews.
Planters and laborers talk of roads, springs and seeding.
Were you there?

Before Pentecost I had known use and disuse
But never before such symbiosis.
Here is no place for a retiring monoculture
Or the cunning of technocrats.

Here present segues to past and towards eternity.
Here is alive with souls who laugh through tears
And those who dance while holding still.
Here is the world for me:
A world where rosewood daughters of surveyors
Fall for piney sons of artisans.
Here is the world for me:
Where bookkeepers and poets share kneelers and sing
Kyrie.
There is no other world for me
But the world of believer and doubter
Drawn irresistibly to the "peace that passeth."
Were you there?

'Protesters'

Green Man Returns

They praise not peace, bending banners
Beneath saw-toothed eyes and spiraling tongues,
Ensnaring everyone in reach of their coiled heads.
Forced from campus, the city, and network news,
I flee to the forest without tent or tarp;
On the seventh day it showers, firm and full of flashes.
I find cover in a canopy of evergreens
And, listening to the lush lure of rain on leaves,
Catch a song syncopated through those stems:
Peace is improbable for screamers:
It's meant for the humblest of hearers.

Golden Hallway

Green Man Returns

Eastern woods at dawn
Are a golden hallway
Where a fox has a den
A bird has a nest
And there is everywhere
For me to rest.

Woodchuck's Repose

Today I walk and climb
Narrow roads in springtime
Between pairs of rocky forest hills,
Where hedges bloom with blue squills.
I search for the waterfall creek
Where you, a salutatory woodchuck,
Raised your head and scurried ahead
Though keeping your distance socially.
Through thinned groves and crevices
You walked before me.
Intact, I find you between two hills, two forests,
Beside the narrow road
Unbruised but for what flowed.
Hit by an ATV or small caliber round—
Others would know, I don't.
Here we are in this trench of green
Wandering where sunlit wind is heard but seldom seen
For on us it never sways
Except at meager moments of the day.
From Adam to today, death is common as clay.
Yet for me it is particular today.

To balance between wisdom and trust…
To avoid the enforced insanity
By saying tragedy is comedy…
To learn that pain should change us
For better and not succumb…
And yet now, what does it mean?
In nature's trench, in this moment's eye,
What is the quintessence of this dream?
Within the mocking carnival encased in green

What means these promises beneath clear sky?

Then light and breeze through chasm shows
A solitary hardwood leaf that glows
Like sunset green shook loose
Across blue space of greenwood gorge.
Then it disappears into weeds and vines
And is seen no more.
Your fur moves and seems to shine
Secure in wisdom all mortality recalls—
Such a difference there is between
One moment and no moment at all.

So much suffering brings us peace
And reminds us of all who were here
And allows us to let go everywhere.
Your end cannot be an end:
Time and memory redeems and commends.
And the difference between
This moment and no moment at all
Between the light and nothingness of the fall—
The readiness of so short a scene—
Is everywhere and everything.

Festival Days

Festivals come
With equinox sun.
So stand still (if you can)
And stand alone
Like a watched deer.
And listen again
Beyond white butterflies:
And laughter, hear
The blue lilies
That speak clear
Of paths unshown
But not unknown.
This is yours—
These the doors.
So stand still (if you can)
And stand alone
And listen again:
Festivals once come
Are never undone.

Natchez Ghosts

1.
Years ago I drove
These parkway spirals
On Good Friday
When rosebuds and dogwoods
Were in infant bloom
And fragrant honeysuckle
Floated like a halo overhead.
The hot disquietude of August noontide
Has leaves shading much
From Southern heat.
The Mississippi winter was wet:
It raged and writhed creeks
Swelling them to woody brooks
And tannic ravines.
Green blades and songbirds
On mossy branches declare what ought to be
Ease of summertime.
But ghosts bewray the holiday—
Phantoms of native peoples,
Kaintucks, and prehistoric beasts
Manifest themselves as markers.
Do wraiths of highwaymen
Drift among trees?
Do specters of boatmen
Upbraid the living?

2.
Signposts declare an Old Trace piece.
I pull aside the car, walk into woods
And search for ways deepened

By untold years and feet
That sought taverns, inns, trading post,
Or forgotten lands for grazing.
Beyond the sunken path
A clearing unveils an old farmhouse
That tightropes before floodplain forests:
A structure planked and square-framed,
Flaunting a prized chimney.
I move towards, but stop
At sunlight's edge to consider
How such pathways
Were shadeless and lined
With cotton or cow pastures.
Now southern pines
Cool fallow lands.
I want ghosts of farmhands
Spirits of husbandmen and farmwives.
They are not here.
Sharecropping and crop-lien were hard.
'Did we put by enough?'
Autumn anxieties were hard.
Did our grandparents spare us
When they surrendered?
Wind beneath loblolly branches repine.
Grumbles of cool breezes
Humble me to look again
At foot-smoothed loess hills,
Hand-pressed alluvial fields.
Winds die and songs of katydids
Pick up from the farmhouse
Through branches and reeds to say,
"Time to drive on.
Not much farther."

3.
Bluffs in the distance
Become kudzu-wreathen—
Invasive vines dome to doom
Natchez trees and hilltops:
Coiling, climbing, and choking,
Suffocating what is made to live.
I reach Rocky Springs' signpost:
"1860, population 2616;
Population today, 0."
I walk the ghost town
With cisterns and safe boxes,
A playground for deer, coyotes,
Occasional skunks, until I reach
The natural footstool on the trail
With its historical plaque:
A history of deserted township—
Civil War, Yellow Fever, erosion, boll weevils.
Was ever this land
For the living?
If ghosts travel the Natchez Trace
Could they dwell only here?

4.
Above is a pillared bluff
With its abandoned parish and churchyard
Besieged by old-growth trees.
Casual whistles of waterthrushes
Surround me as I walk
Upward towards a disused church.
The brick building is a simple structure
With prominent placement. At the doors
Flycatchers and warblers are loud.
They seem to say,

"He comes from dead lands.
Though dead, their race has cunning.
Beware, beware, beware!"
Then breezes of brightness
Pierce the mossy shade.
A white dazzle where
It's too shaded for sun
Engulfs me in bright pallor
And all is translucent.
The skin of soul is bare
Before gracious light that comes
Out of darkness.
The dead neither haunt nor clamor here.
I am a ghost from ghostly races:
All else lives but me, and I am afraid
Like those who followed him
Into the Transfiguration.
When they went upward,
Did they think their fish
Their nets, boats, or taxes
Was *real life*?
It seemed a dream or retreat
As they followed trancelike
Up the mountain until
They were frightened with truth
That their lives before them
Had been a daydream:
A half-life in shadow of full.
Awakened and aware,
They were ghosts
Among the living.

5.
I have words
Though life and strength
Are borrowed.
Above ruins of town,
Beneath church and old-growth leaves
I am thin and clear
Before a whitening flame.
Let me not dissolve.
T.S. Eliot asked to be taught
To sit still, to care and not care…
Teach me to distinguish between reality and time…
Teach me to discern difference
Between optimism and hope…
Create in me wakefulness;
Do not allow clouds of temporal tense
To overshadow me;
Do not cast me with cunning vapors
But renew my experience with wisdom
To say what is not easy to say.
Take the veil from wearied eyes
And give me glimpses of renewed creation
To sustain me as I traverse
These deadman's lands.

Portrait of the Lady

Inspired by Alice Havers

1.
Inside Norwich Castle museum
Pretentious passersby draw me
Towards the oiled canvas:
Someone says, "Young Gloria Swanson."
Rambling ensues on *Sunset Boulevard.*
On they walk.

I see fig limbs in summer foliage
With espaliered branches
Grown into a window
Shading maiden and child.
At enervated feet
Falls premature
The solitary leaf.
A long index finger
Attempts to deflect
Attention from her to him.
Her heightened love holds
What is bright and anointed.
Her coiffure, eventide disheveled,
Retains a monody splendor.
Loamy circles she wears
As eyeshadow of maidenhood.
Terraqueous eyes flow with thoughts
Pensive and fecund.
But what thoughts?
An hour nap before feeding? Changing?
Her ruminations compound and rivet:
She is wheels on a clock;

She cannot sleep.

2.
She has forgotten to remove
The filigreed bracelet
From the night before;
This postprandial rest
Is his longest in days.
A hard twelve hours it's been:
Life, death, life—*My soul,*
Can all be mere death and putrescence?

Gears of thought
Tick and turn.
With motherly perspicacity
She stolidly reflects
On frustrations and lack of sleep:
This is pilulous comfort.
Loneliness she's known:
Bright girl of the village,
Flexuous in figure;
Beautiful, though boys feared
To see (except distantly).
Books, lessons, and songs
Were a sequestrate comfort;
But no protection from
Superincumbent loneliness.
She wanted to be as others.
Something never let her.

He stirs.
Her long fingers
Ascend to sooth.

Thoughts, visions belabor her:
Aftergrasses of Nazareth;
Bethlehem in afterlight;
Egyptian riverscapes and arid hinterlands:
Now home again.
Her wanderings cannot, will not, cease.
Loneliness she's faced.

3.
No restless child
But a fig leaf's fall
Sets such minds
To crystalline reason
And corrugated feelings;
Budding figs, buzzing wasps,
Force her to ponder futures
Where like Lear
And his Cordelia
She finds herself
Where wisdom and premonitions
Cannot console.

She holds him
And holds away visions
Of battered nature
That pelt her heart.
I hear her proclaim,
"Never, never, never, never."
She could teach Shakespeare such lines:
"Why should a dog,
A horse, a rat have life,
and thou no breath at all?"

She would weep and wail

Had this night not hitherto
Leathered her quiescent:
At dawn she lacks her voice
And previous plangent tears.
Yet she holds him
As close as she will again:
A glimpse for Michelangelo's Pieta.
That time is not now:
Joy remains before them.

4.
She recalls the night,
Holding and holding him
And suffering household whispers
Of those who neither know nor love.
"Something is wrong," they said.
"How he screams.
The mistress spoils him;
Some idiot he is.
She's too inexperienced;
She needs a real nurse.
Remember how pretty she was?
And book smart, at least.
Our village women know better.
They have more sense.
What can she know?"

Her aqueous gaze
Traces a photosphere
Towards that horizon
She cannot wish away;
There sit the green hills.
Yet unmerited love
Conceives more love,

And she learns love
In ways not understood.
Love is what she holds—
A peony confluence for
All passions and philosophies.
All morning night she holds him
And holds him to let him go.

5.
Maiden and child
Browsed in a museum:
Two subjects, still and moving.
Forever captured, sainted moment,
Upon oiled canvas:
Pondering maiden, teenage mother,
Holy Queen: a glow from him,
Reveals a regnant face
For whom love is everything.
Such wisdom here!
In ocular pools
She implores all truth!
From nothing
She brought forth love,
And that is all there is!
Light brought forth from nothing
That likewise reveals
Something forgotten, learned anew:
Continuity of love
Is old and always new.
Through the years to come
May the Holy Queen
Continue her vigil
In Norwich Castle museum;
May a stray passerby

Stop and see
Stop and praise
The one who
For a sleepless night
Held for us
All summer,
All hopes
All love
In mortal hands.

Note: Alice Havers (1850-1890) was a 19th century English painter and illustrator. As a child, she lived for a time in the Falkland Islands and in South America. Havers had three children with Frederick Morgan, her husband who was himself an acclaimed artist. Havers divorced Morgan 2 years before her death. The inspiration for this poem is Havers' oil on canvas entitled "But Mary kept all these things and pondered them in her heart" (1888). The painting hangs in Norwich Castle Museum. The image can be found easily on the internet.

Our Corner

For Lucy

Aside outdoor fire-ring
    By light fed from autumn
Our poetry club reads
    Shakespeare's seventy-third.

Or a rented Florida villa
    Where we reconvene
Behind sunset-bathed windows
    Where green palms unfist
To hold blue air
    With briny breeze.
You say, "Next poem, please."
    We reenact *Tempest* under moonrise
Opposite our window that appears
    In likeness of lighted conch.
Before nightfall, we declare
    "Full fathom five thy father lies"
As ocean outside traverses
    And pulls and pumps
Boundaries of time, hearts of worlds.

Or a future when we drive
    Westward and stop between
Texas and California before nightfall
    To watch Umbopa and Quatermain
Stand on sands of golden brown against
    Pink-washed wilderness sky.

Then come Saturday visits
      Within an autism faculty where
We delve into Helen Farris's
      Favorite Poems, Old and New.
Between locked doors
      Secured within walls
We read of seasons, family,
      Friends, country, fancies,
Beginnings, beasts, how to play…
      Ours this is: a poet's corner.

Hold Summer

For Lucy

I remember Ship Island summers—
A boy barefoot for the day
Free to traverse sandy edges of the world
Where dolphins and stingrays glided beside him
And hermit crabs filled the Gulf floor.
What did I know?
But where sun and sky meet a continental shelf,
I could hold summer in my hand and be anything.
Now I watch sands beneath your feet
Give way to waves and give the waves away.
Sea lords stoop to hand you a hermit crab:
I don't always know what is true;
But against 'reality' I cannot doubt
No one can stop you—
You can be anything:
You hold summer in your hand.

Butterfly House

Fritillaries and swallowtails
Wave from nectar wands,
And zebra longwing couples seem
More into themselves than us.
We see winged malachite
Above other flora of the air.
Within cool and netted spheres—
Partition to partition, net to net—
The world is a window suncatcher;
Around us everywhere are colors of air.
All is a Tiffany lamp:
A sunbeam, translucent and alive.
In refractive glow, let us recall
Time's pace, fluttery loss,
Memory's filament, iridescent life:
In a single moment, all summer
Inside a place where everything
Whispers of promise, and everywhere
Promises are possible.

CONVERSATIONS

Interview with Dr. Jonathan Sircy

JONATHAN SIRCY: How do you decide that a certain topic—if you want to write about Mississippi, for instance—deserves to be in a poetic form versus a prose form? What are you able to do in poetry when you're writing about place that prose can't do?

CHAD CHISHOLM: A lot of times my prose is looking at an experience that I had about my education. I just had an article published recently about my grammatical instruction. Obviously, I kind of knew where I was going with that. When I write prose, the ending is more important than the thesis I start out with because that can change, but I usually know where I want it to end. When it is poetry, there's some sort of effect, some core, some sort of feeling and intuition I have, and I'm not sure what it means. And these are the poems where I explore what I don't always know, at least not from my first drafts. I suppose when I write a piece of prose, it's about what I want you to think. When I write a poem, it's more about what I want you to feel.

SIRCY: Are you somebody who feels something all the time about places like Mississippi, or is it only occasionally when you have the sort of feelings you're talking about being the generative force for poetry?

CHISHOLM: I obviously don't write about everywhere that I go. I don't have these intuitions, these aspirations, for every place.

In *Mad Men*, Don Draper says to Peggy Olson, "The product is all about what you feel." And there is something to that with poetry for me when I write about a place. You go back to Wordsworth, *Preface to Lyrical Ballads*. You visit a place; that's what you feel, what you're inspired by; or maybe it's what you are bringing with you to the place. And the place has the answer; it unearths something that needed to come out; that's usually how a place works with me.

SIRCY: Let's talk about your poem on the Natchez Trace. Did *that* place give you an answer? Did it provoke questions?

CHISHOLM: It provoked a lot of questions. Very much so. The Natchez Trace—I've known it for a long time. It's an interesting little drive. It's not really on the way to anything. It's just a leisurely kind of drive to take. And there's always markers that invite reflection. You stop at a road sign or a stop at a trading post if you want to soak in history.

The poem is about ghosts, so there's a lot of ghosts. There's these hauntings, which is not to say I believe the Trace is literally haunted, although some people do believe that. There are legends. But I guess when it comes to me, like a lot of people who are drawn to poetry, I'm drawn to tradition and interested in traditions.

I'm interested in ancestors of people that have come before us. The ancestor is kind of like a ghost, or traditions are like ghosts: it's always present, even if it's unsubstantial at times. You're not sure what to make of it. I like to explore that in going to places and learning about true traditions or history. It does invoke poetry sometimes, sometimes good poetry.

SIRCY: Is that how you experience South Carolina?

CHISHOLM: Yes. I think a lot of my best poetry has actually been about South Carolina. I could go through a couple of poems of mine.

I recently wrote a poem called "Skies of Seas," one of the longer poems that I've written. It takes place on Roper Mountain with my daughter Lucy, at the Roper Mountain pinnacle overlooking the city and all the things that happened there, at the science center. I wrote a poem that was published in *St. Austin's Review* about St. Paul's Episcopal Church in Pendleton. I finished a poem not too long ago about the solar eclipse that I experienced in South Carolina.

It's odd, because I'm not a native of South Carolina, though I've lived here for eight years total. I wasn't really a native of Mississippi either. My mom was born on the West Coast. I was born on the West Coast, but I was raised in Mississippi. I've written quite a bit about South Carolina and probably going to continue. This has become like home.

SIRCY: So, when you do that, are you always trying to invoke your own perspective, convey that to the reader, or are you adopting a persona that you're writing from?

CHISHOLM: It's a different part of myself, I suppose, but it is me channeling that persona or perspective. In *Surprised by Joy*, C.S. Lewis talks about consciousness and how there's a difference between "I" and "me." He uses the two personal pronouns, and he distinguishes between the two sides of himself. I think there is something to that. The conscious "I" goes first—the more objective point of view that looks at the world—and "me," the direct object if you will, that things happened to.

My poetry is probably more the subconscious "me." And that's the part of me that really experiences a place, where the "I" of existence has retreated a little bit to absorb what I see. So when I recall an experience, this leads me to change little things in my poems. In the poem about seeing the solar eclipse with my daughter, I changed the setting a little bit instead of being on the campus of Southern Wesleyan University. I just picture that hilltop and a lot of astronomy people, people who were interested in science, not so much faith, to sort of explore that event in a different way.

SIRCY: Where do you get your theological understanding of place from?

CHISHOLM: Whether it's Dante taking a not very literal journey but a metaphysical one, or the idea of a journey and keeping your eyes open and things happening to you along the road—I've picked up a lot [of theology] from that entire body of literature that deals with this spiritual journey without really even knowing where it came from.

One thing I've been thinking about is the Old Testament, how that begins with the patriarchs encountering the sacred and then building a shrine and altar there. And that place became sacred because of that encounter. It became sacred not just for them and their family, but for the entire nation.

Then there was the Deuteronomic reform where they tore down all these little shrines. Instead they focused all worship in Jerusalem. But, Christianity came around later, and one of the early popes said if people are worshipping at a tree, don't curse the tree. Baptize the tree and use that as a way to teach people. I think of St. Patrick and Ireland and how a lot of churches that he planted were at pagan meeting places. They realized something and discovered that people could meet God there. Here they would minister, and they would transform these places. The pagan waters were transformed into baptismal waters.

When we give a place metaphysical or sacred significance, it becomes more than just that hill or a clump of trees. Every generation has to find it for themselves, but they can as long as we keep teaching them through our poems and through our stories.

SIRCY: Can you give us a preview of what you're going to talk about at the festival?

CHISHOLM: The presentation will run the gamut of my work. Obviously, metaphysical truth is really important to me. And despite the different themes, the different poems that I'll be reading, they'll be full of metaphysical truth, which is important to me.

SIRCY: We're looking forward to it!

CHISHOLM: Thank you so much!

Lucy at the local science center.

THE AUTHOR

A BRIEF NOTE

CHAD CHISHOLM is a professor at Southern Wesleyan University in South Carolina where he teaches writing, rhetoric, and literature. For his work in the classroom, he has received awards such as the Exemplary Teacher Award from the United Methodist Board of Higher Education. Two of his previous books, *Clinton* and *Clinton: 1940-1980*, are with Arcadia Publishing. His essay collection, *Requiems and Reveries*, was published by Freedom's Hill Press. Chisholm also has publications in journals as diverse as *Mississippi Folklife*, *The South Carolina Review*, *Connecticut Review*, *Mallorn: The Journal of the J.R.R. Tolkien Society*, *The Mississippi Encyclopedia*, *Saint Austin Review*, *Classis Quarterly Journal*, and *Mythlore: A Journal of J.R.R. Tolkien, C.S. Lewis, Charles Williams, and Mythopoeic Literature*. He lives with his family on the outskirts of Greenville, South Carolina.